Family in the Fifties

Alison Hurst

A & C Black · London

Black's Junior Reference Books
General Editor R J Unstead

Hurst, Alison
  Family in the Fifties.–(Black's junior
reference books)
  1. Great Britain–Social life and customs–
20th century–Juvenile literature
  I. Title
  941.085'5   DA566.4

  ISBN 0–7136–2703–4

Published by A & C Black (Publishers) Limited
35 Bedford Row, London WC1R 4JH

© 1987 A & C Black (Publishers) Limited
First published 1987

Every effort has been made to trace and acknowledge copyright owners. If any right has been omitted, the publishers offer their apologies and will rectify this in subsequent editions following notification.

Typeset by August Filmsetting, Haydock, St Helens.
Printed in Great Britain by R J Acford Ltd, Chichester, Sussex.

Contents

Introduction

What do you imagine when you think of the 1950s? You may think of rock'n'roll music, winklepicker shoes or perhaps a great occasion like the Coronation of Queen Elizabeth II. Your grandparents, and perhaps your parents too, lived through this decade.

Edward Turner had been 18 when World War II began, and went to serve in the Army about half way through the war. His girlfriend, Eileen, worked in a munitions factory during the war. Through the years Edward was away, he and Eileen wrote many letters to each other.

Many people lost members of their family and loved ones in the war. Edward and Eileen were overjoyed to be together again in 1946, and in this book you can read about what life was like in Britain during the 1950s for the Turner family and some of their friends.

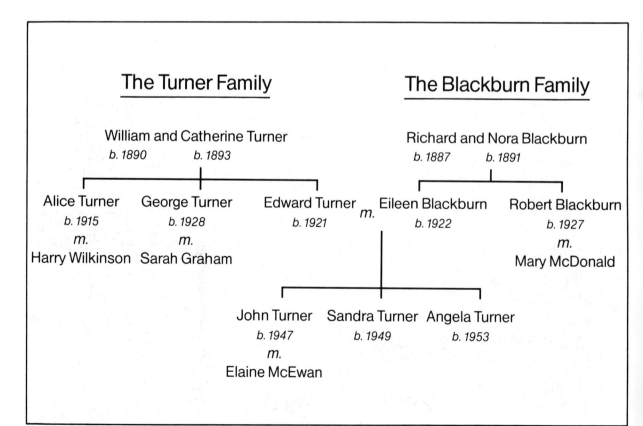

The Turner Family

William and Catherine Turner
b. 1890   b. 1893

Alice Turner   George Turner   Edward Turner
b. 1915   b. 1928   b. 1921
m.   m.
Harry Wilkinson   Sarah Graham

m.

The Blackburn Family

Richard and Nora Blackburn
b. 1887   b. 1891

Eileen Blackburn   Robert Blackburn
b. 1922   b. 1927
                         m.
                         Mary McDonald

John Turner   Sandra Turner   Angela Turner
b. 1947   b. 1949   b. 1953
m.
Elaine McEwan

1   A new start

The Turner family

In May 1945, World War Two ended, and everyone felt that new and better times were just beginning. When Edward Turner left the army in 1946, he asked his childhood sweetheart, Eileen Blackburn, to marry him. The following year the wedding took place.

Edward:
'I was very lucky. Some of my friends had been killed or badly injured in the war. I came out of it in one piece, Eileen was waiting for me and I managed to get a good job.'

There was no chance of a grand wedding for the young couple. During the war, and for some time afterwards, food and clothes were rationed. Rationed goods could only be bought with coupons which were issued by the government. Each person was only allowed a limited number of coupons.

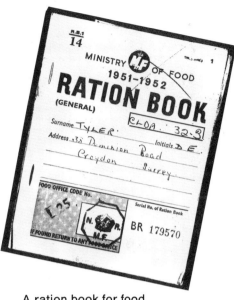

A ration book for food

Edward and Eileen on their wedding day

5

Eileen:

'There were 32 guests at the reception – this was the most we were allowed. I think it was something to do with the hotel catering. We had boiled ham and salad, and everyone had a glass of sherry to drink. You can't imagine what luxury this was, with rationing at its height.'

Eileen was fortunate with her wedding dress. Her mother had saved some material from before the war. There was such a shortage of material at this time that some brides even wore dresses made up from wartime parachute silk.

What a contrast between Edward and Eileen's wedding presents and the sort of gifts some newly-married couples receive today! After the war, nearly everything was in short supply, and no luxury items, such as crystal glasses, were available. Some people even gave Edward and Eileen things from their own homes, because there were so few suitable presents to buy in the shops.

Eileen:

'We didn't have much by today's standards, but as we were starting out with nothing, anything was welcome!'

Some fifties chair designs

Utility furniture – well-made but plain

A lot of furniture, clothes and other goods had a 'Utility' mark. Although the goods were plainly designed, the Utility mark was a guarantee that an article was of high quality even though it was not expensive. The Government introduced 'Utility' goods for newly-married couples, or families whose homes had been destroyed by bombs in the war. Edward and Eileen still have a little jug with the 'Utility' mark, which always comes out when their grandchildren have tea with them.

During the war years not many houses had been built, and many existing homes badly needed modernising. Even in 1960 there were 17 million people in Britain (out of a population of 46 million) living in houses without baths or hot water. The housing shortage of the 1950s made life difficult for newly-married couples like Edward and Eileen. There was no hope of getting a house straight away, so they had to move in with Eileen's parents.

The house Eileen grew up in

A utility label from one of Edward's shirts

The proud new father – Edward with baby John

Eileen:

'Lots of young couples at that time started married life in their parents' homes, and we felt quite happy about this. It was more difficult after our baby, John, was born. Like most babies, he made a lot of noise, and suddenly my parents' house seemed too small for us all!'

The next spring the young family were delighted to be able to move into a home of their own – 24 Rustington Road, Oakley. This road was part of a large estate of new houses built after the war. Just over a year after moving into their new house, Edward and Eileen's second baby, Sandra, was born.

Rustington Road, Oakley. A lot of new houses were built after the war. Edward and Eileen thought their new house was luxurious

The logo for the Festival of Britain appeared everywhere in 1951. Many companies used it to boost their own sales

The Festival of Britain

In 1951 the Festival of Britain took place in London. It lasted for five months and was a huge event, made up of many exciting exhibitions. Its purpose was to show what incredible progress the country had made since the beginning of the Second World War, and also to cheer up the British people, after the hard times they had just lived through.

In the years leading up to the Festival there had been many scientific and technological advances in Britain. Inside the Dome of Discovery, for example, visitors could find out about penicillin, a new drug which had saved many lives during the war. Other interesting exhibits included the world's first turbo-jet engine.

Young people like Edward and Eileen were particularly interested in the daring interior decorations and furniture designs, with their bright, vivid colours and unfamiliar shapes. Soon, these ideas were being copied in homes throughout Britain.

Edward:
'Eileen and I had great fun when we visited the festival. There were all kinds of entertainments apart from the exhibitions. I remember open-air cafes and fantastic fun fairs. We took back a set of Festival of Britain pencils for John – he still has one left today!'

Emigration: New opportunities abroad

Although the Festival of Britain had brightened things up, and life was slowly beginning to improve, a lot of people still felt unhappy and unsettled, after the war.

During the 1950s, many people felt they would be better off in Australia or Canada rather than staying in Britain with its shortages and high taxes. Thousands decided to start new lives abroad, among them Edward's sister Alice and her husband Harry, who emigrated to Canada in 1956. Harry had been impressed by life abroad when he was posted overseas with the Air Force, during the war. He wanted his family to have a fresh start in another country. It was exciting for Alice, but old Mr and Mrs Turner were heartbroken when their daughter went abroad.

The Festival of Britain on London's South Bank, showing the Dome of Discovery and Skylon

The 'caterpillar' was only one of the attractions at the opening of Battersea Fun Fair in 1956

Edward:

'I felt very sorry for my parents, but I also saw Alice and Harry's point of view. The war years, and those just after, had been dismal, and a very rosy picture was painted of the future in Canada. I would have been tempted to go myself, if it hadn't been for the fact that I had a really good job and my family was happily settled. We had too much to lose here in Britain to uproot ouselves.'

Air travel

Alice and Harry travelled to Canada in a huge ocean liner. At the beginning of the 1950s, travel by sea was the main way to visit foreign countries. By the end of the 1950s, aeroplanes had become the most important means of international travel.

Trans-Atlantic routes were badly affected by the new importance of air travel, and many famous liners that had dominated the Atlantic for years, such as the 'Queen Mary' and the 'Queen Elizabeth' eventually ceased travelling this route.

A family discussing emigration with an official at Australia House in London. Many families looked for a new future in the Commonwealth countries

Air travel at this time was mainly for the rich and famous, and quite beyond the reach of ordinary people. In August 1946, BEA (British European Airways) was formed and, in its first month, 9 300 passengers were carried. Ten years later this number of passengers was carried every day. By the end of the 1950s, BEA was flying more than five million people a year.

On May 3rd 1952, the first jet airliner service opened when a BOAC (British Overseas Airways Corporation) Comet flew from London to Johannesburg (6 726 miles) in $23\frac{1}{2}$ hours, at a speed of 345 mph. This flight cut the prevous time by half.

Eileen:
'When we got married, we would have found it difficult to believe that, by the time we had grandchildren, flying would be a familiar way to travel.'

Passenger aircraft were small and uncomfortable. Air travel was still a novelty

11

A new queen

In February 1952 King George VI died when he was only 56 years old. George VI's elder daughter was crowned Queen Elizabeth II in June 1953. All kinds of celebrations were planned, from tea parties to huge banquets.

The Coronation was the first State occasion to be televised, and the whole country seemed to be in a fever of excitement. The Turners spent the day with their neighbours, Jean and Bill Francis.

Eileen:
'Coronation Day was like a party in their house, as they had one of the first televisions in the neighbourhood. Several families managed to cram into their front room, so that we could all watch this historic event as it actually happened. Our second daughter, Angela, was born shortly before the Coronation, so the whole day was, for us, like an extra celebration for our new baby!'

Neighbourhood parties were held right across the country to celebrate the crowning of the young Queen, and people looked forward to the start of a new Elizabethan age.

A Coronation tea party in Camden Town, London. Each child was given a Coronation mug to keep

2 The Turners' home

At the Turners' house in Rustington Road there have been many changes since the 1950s. The kitchen has altered a lot since those days. Then, their kitchen sink was porcelain, and had a wooden draining board attached to it at either side. Both the sink and the draining board had to be scrubbed hard to keep them clean.

The kitchen floor was covered in linoleum (lino), a very popular form of floor covering at that time. It was fairly cheap, easy to put down and to keep clean.

Most people had not heard of kitchen units at the beginning of the 1950s.

Eileen:
'We had a larder where most of the food was stored, and a tall cupboard where I kept my cleaning equipment. The room was painted green and cream – this was the height of fashion for kitchens in those days. We sometimes ate our meals at the kitchen table, but I remember hoping that nobody would catch us eating in there – at that time it didn't seem the 'proper' thing to do at all!'

Eileen was keen to replace her old kitchen (below) with new fitted units (above)

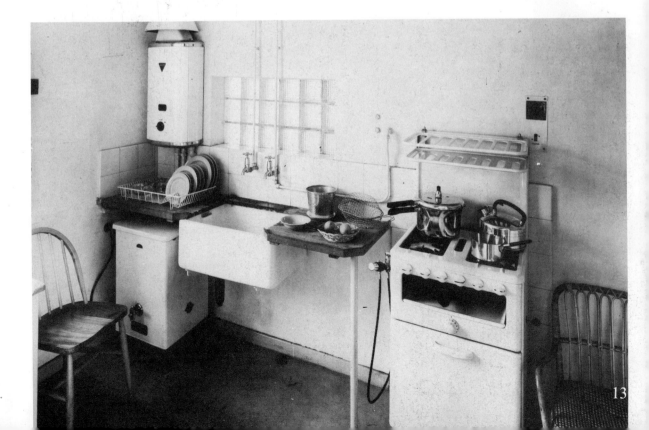

13

In the days before fridges, food was kept cool in a meat safe

Refrigerators were rapidly becoming more common in the 1950s, but most people still used a 'meat safe' – kept in the coolest part of the larder to keep food fresh.

Eileen was pleased to have an electric cooker in the new house, as these were considered very modern and up-to-date. Electricity in homes had only become common in the 1930s. When Eileeen had her first electric washing machine she was delighted – washing everything by hand had been a time-consuming chore.

Sandra:
'Mum talks about all the work that the washing machine saved her, but I remember washing day being a lot of hard work. Even with an electric wringer, you had to feed the clothes in by hand – there was water dripping all over the place! Then, in winter, all the damp clothes would be hoisted up on a pulley above the kitchen to dry.'

An early fifties electric washing machine. All the clothes had to be fed through the mangle by hand

It was considered very 'contemporary' to match constrasting designs of wallpaper, carpet and curtains. Another favourite feature for designers were decorative 'cocktail cherries', seen here decorating coat hooks

During the 1950s, many homes had telephones installed for the first time. There was often a very long waiting list and it was three years before the Turners got their telephone.

John:
'Most telephone numbers at that time were short, because there weren't nearly as many telephones as there are now. Our number was Oakley 942. To make a long distance 'phone call you had to go through the operator, and give the name of the place you were calling, and then the number.'

Before the war, carpets and wallpapers had often been in subdued greens and browns with pleasant, although unexciting, floral designs. The Festival of Britain started a new fashion for bright colours and bold patterns in home furnishings. A word that was popular at the time to describe something really up-to-date and fashionable, was 'contemporary'. The Turners thought all the brightly coloured and patterned furnishings a bit shocking at first.

Whether Contemporary or traditional...

Carpets make a home

Geometric designs, inspired by artists of the time, like Klee, were typical of the Fifties

Some special features of a fifties living room: wicker plant pot, wrought iron plant stand, wall lights, contrasting geometric designs and a feeling of space

Edward:

'When our friends Ron and Joyce decorated their front room with three walls covered in one wallpaper and the fourth wall in a different paper, Eileen and I didn't like it at all. A year or so later, when we came to decorate our lounge, we decided to have one wall papered differently so that our room was 'contemporary' as well. I suppose this shows how quickly new fashions catch on.'

Fitted carpets, in a variety of 'contemporary' designs, were becoming popular by the late 1950s. The Turners, however, had square carpets in the centre of their rooms, surrounded by lino or stained and polished floorboards. Only a few people could afford to buy all the latest comforts and fashions for their homes.

Sandra:

'A lot of our furniture was old. I used to do my homework curled up on our ancient sofa – it was so comfortable and the wide arms made good 'rests' for my books. Our old sofa was so huge it took up most of the lounge.'

Edward and Eileen were especially proud of some new light fittings they had bought. They had a fashionable 'contemporary' shape, and were fixed on the walls. Today, Edward and Eileen still have these lights.

After tea, in the living room

Angela:
'I think Mum and Dad's wall-lights are great – they remind me of when I was little! Some people probably think they look old-fashioned, but to me it just wouldn't seem right if their house was full of new, modern things.'

There was a craze for indoor plants.

Eileen:
'Lots of my friends started buying indoor plants, and we all had fancy plant stands to show them off in. All that wrought ironwork used to get dusty, but it was lovely to have greenery about the house.'

Bedrooms were furnished quite simply, often with heavy dark furniture. Blankets and white cotton or linen sheets were usual, and a shiny eiderdown or candlewick bedspread to cover the bed.

Central heating was still rare, but many people replaced coal fires with gas and electric heaters.

Although the solid darkwood furniture is quite heavy looking, there is lots of space and light in this fifties bedroom

A typical fifties dressing table

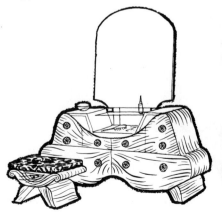

17

The bathroom – is this anything like the bathroom in your house? All lavatories had a tank high up on the wall

Eileen:

'When we moved into our house, we had coal fires in the downstairs rooms every day in the cold weather. This was what we had been used to all our lives, and our parents before us. My grandchildren think this sounds wonderful, but it was a dirty, messy job each morning, cleaning out the old fire and re-making and lighting it, and the house was freezing cold until they were lit. When the new electric heaters came into the shops I could hardly wait to buy one. I must say I did enjoy the luxury of heat at the flick of a switch.'

Eileen and Edward thought that one of the best features of 24 Rustington Road was its bathroom, although it would seem a very plain, bare place compared with most modern bathrooms. In those days, many houses still had an outside toilet and no proper bathroom. The Turners' bathroom had a standard bathroom suite – bath, basin and lavatory – which was available only in white.

John:

'What I remember most was getting up on a cold winter morning. It was freezing, standing on the icy bathroom floor, getting washed – if you were the last one to use the bathroom you often got cold water too, as the others would have used up all the hot!'

The water was heated by a coke-fired boiler in the kitchen, and once the tank was empty it took a long time to heat up again.

An all-in-one cooker and water heater advert from the Fifties

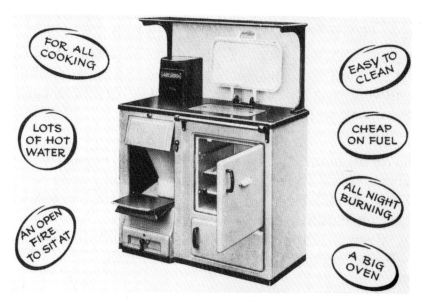

FOR ALL COOKING

EASY TO CLEAN

LOTS OF HOT WATER

CHEAP ON FUEL

ALL NIGHT BURNING

AN OPEN FIRE TO SIT AT

A BIG OVEN

During the 1950s, the Turners found that their eating habits changed. The end of rationing meant that food such as oranges or bananas, which had rarely been available, were again back in the shops. Some types of fruit and vegetables had to be imported, which usually meant that they were expensive. Many more varieties of tinned food were becoming available, but the growth in canned produce was not nearly as great as the boom in deep-frozen food.

People would buy frozen food even if they didn't have a fridge. This was quite safe if the food was used soon after being bought. As refrigerator sales soared, the sales of frozen food also grew.

Buying their first fridge in 1958 made a big difference to the Turners.

Eileen:
'Before we had the fridge, we ate a lot of stews in winter, with carrots, parsnips and other vegetables that were in season. Of course, we didn't stop eating this sort of food, but with the fridge, most vegetables never went out of season! It was a great treat to be able to store special foods like ice-cream at home as well.'

After the end of rationing, it was wonderful to be able to have fruit from abroad again

The Turner family all remember what a luxury it was to eat chicken. In those days, chickens weren't kept in huge battery farms as they are now, so chicken was very expensive. Joints of meat, however, were quite cheap compared with today.

John:
'We used to have a roast joint every Sunday without fail – usually roast beef with Yorkshire pudding. If we had roast chicken it was a very special treat. Today it's the other way round. We have chicken all the time, but if my wife cooks a joint of beef it's something we really appreciate.'

At the beginning of the 1950s the Turners still had their milk delivered in a horse-drawn milk float. There was a big advertising campaign at this time to get people, especially children, to drink more milk, as it contains valuable calcium and vitamins.

Milk puddings were very much a part of the week's menu.

Angela:
'Most meals finished off with a hot pudding – treacle sponge, Spotted Dick, or one of many others. I liked them all apart from the milk puddings, which I thought were horrible. Mum didn't make me eat them, thank goodness, as we were always eating semolina and rice pudding at school.'

A famous film star, Norman Wisdom, was used in adverts for milk

Milk was still often delivered by a horse-drawn milk float

3 Shopping

Food

Many of the food shops in the Turners' neighbourhood were changing. During the war years self-service shops had been almost unheard of.

Then, in the early 1950s, supermarkets began to open up all over the country. By 1955 there were about 3000 of these new shops in Britain and, soon after, as many as 50 new supermarkets were being opened each month.

Eileen:
'I remember when our local Co-op store changed over to self-service. It was difficult to find what you wanted at first, but I soon began to prefer this way of shopping – it was certainly faster! One thing I missed was a chat with the assistant behind the counter. Self-service is definitely not such a friendly way of shopping.'

Although many people regretted the arrival of self-service shops, they certainly speeded up shopping

The fashion floor of this department store is very like the one at Kents. The displays were formal and look stiff and unnatural today

Department and chain stores

Before the war most people had shopped at small, specialist shops or at large, independent department stores such as Kents which was a family business. Edward's children loved to go with him to Kents, where he worked.

Sandra:

'It was wonderful, like stepping into a different world. A snack in the store cafeteria was a real treat. There were crisp white tablecloths, and waitresses who brought my mother's tea in an elegant pot, and my glass of milk on a saucer.'

During the 1950s millions of pounds were spent redesigning department stores in order to display goods more effectively. As there was more money around to be spent, shops were competing with one another to attract customers.

It was a special treat to have tea in a department store cafeteria

The most important change in the High Street was the rise of the chain store. Chain stores have a number of branches, all with the same name and the same management. Woolworths was one of the first successful chain stores, and in the 1950s most towns had an established branch of 'Woolies'.

Sandra:
'If you wanted your pocket money to go a long way, you went to Woolworths, where there were masses of different things which cost as little as 6d (2½p) each.'

Marks and Spencer is a chain store which acquired a 'new image' in the 1950s. At that time they concentrated mainly on clothing. Their sweaters were about half the price of similar garments in other shops, and were extremely good value for money.

The very first branches of Woolworths divided all goods into 6d and 3d. However after the war prices had to be increased

The government ended
restrictions on hire purchase
in 1958. Firms were able to sell
goods on easier terms with
smaller deposits

Hire purchase

Many shops at this time offered 'hire purchase' credit
terms. This meant that instead of paying for goods all in
one go, people could pay a little bit every week until
they had paid the full price. A survey in 1953 showed
that almost one family in four was paying for something on hire purchase. In 1956 another survey showed
that half the television sets and one-third of vacuum
cleaners were bought on HP.

Eileen:
'Before I got married, it was generally thought to be rather
shameful to buy something on HP – or the 'never, never' as it
was sometimes called. People didn't like to admit that
they hadn't enough money to afford to buy things outright.
Gradually, HP became more widespread, and by the end of
the 1950s it was just another thing that had become part of
our lives.'

4 Getting about

Public transport

A lot of people travelled by bus at the beginning of the 1950s, but there were still many tram services all over the country. In 1950 there were 800 trams left in London. 'Last Tram Week', in London, was in July 1952.

Eileen:
'There was quite a fuss made about the last tram service in London – it was in the papers and on the radio news. We had trams round our way for a few years after that; the children always used to enjoy a ride on them. It was sad to see them go.'

The railway stations were never the same again after the 1950s. It was the end of the Age of Steam for the railways, which, after the war, never regained the importance they once had. British Railways ignored diesel and electric trains at first, and spent a lot of money on new designs of steam locomotive.

When diesels at last began to replace the old steam trains, third class carriages disappeared too.

In the Fifties, each tiny village or town had its own station. The train was used for short trips as much as for long journeys

Ron's 1935 Lanchester
drop-head coupé

John:

'It was a real shame when the steam trains went. When I was a boy my grandad and I would sometimes go train spotting. It was really exciting watching the old trains roaring along, belting out clouds of smoke.'

Cars

With the end of petrol rationing in 1950, and the incomes of many families steadily rising, more and more people were buying cars. Before the war there had been just over three million motor vehicles in Britain. At the end of the 1950s this figure had risen to ten million. All over the country, roads were transformed by the huge increase in number of cars. Traffic jams became a new hazard.

Edward couldn't afford a car in the 1950s, but his friend Ron Atkins managed to save up for one.

Ron:

'I bought a 1935 Lanchester drop-head coupé in 1953. It cost me £145, and I felt really proud to have such a sporty looking car.'

Rush hour traffic in London 1955

Family outing in a Hillman Minx. More cars meant that people started to use them for family outings and picnics

One reason why many people bought older cars was that a large proportion of new cars manufactured in this country were sent abroad for sale, to help boost Britain's exports. The Hillman Minx earned more money through sales abroad than any other single product at this time. Two thousand of these cars were turned out of the factories each week, and more than 60% of these were exported. Other familiar cars of the 1950s included the Ford Consul, Zephyr and Anglia, and the Morris Minor and Oxford. Foreign cars were hardly ever seen.

They're proud of IT!

Zebra crossings were introduced in the Fifties because of
the huge rise in the number of
accidents

Another way to ease the con-
gestion – a bobby directs
the traffic

The increased number of cars caused some unexpect-
ed problems for town planners. Harlow, in Essex, was a
new town built after the war. It had been planned with
one garage to every ten homes. By the time the town
was built, every other home needed a garage! Eventually the big increase in cars on the roads reduced the
number of bus passengers. Buses were also slower in
many areas, due to traffic jams caused by all the new
cars. Less reliable bus services encouraged yet more
people to buy cars, which made the roads even more
congested!

The sudden appearance of so many cars made many
changes in the environment.

Edward:
'In the early 1950s, traffic lights and roundabouts were both
quite unusual sights – you used to see policemen directing
traffic at busy road junctions. Parked cars didn't seem to
clutter streets up too much – there weren't enough of them! I
remember reading something about parking meters in the
local paper. It said that this American idea would never
catch on in Britain, as cars here were made in a far wider
range of sizes!'

5   Changes at work

In the store

When Edward first started work in Kents Department Store in 1936, he earned 15 shillings (75p) a week as a messenger boy. At that time most shops offered training schemes to school leavers.

Edward:
'I expected to stay with the shop all my working life – as it turned out I was quite right! Today's shops don't offer a fraction of the old sort of training to young employees, but then most young shop assistants probably won't stay in the same job as long as I did.'

After the war, Edward returned to Kents, where he began a thorough re-training scheme as a sales assistant in the menswear department. By 1955 he had been promoted to Assistant Buyer, when he earned £10 2s 6d (£10.12) per week. In the 1950s there were often quite strict rules and regulations regarding employees' behaviour, as this extract from the staff rule book for Kents for 1955 shows:

'Your reception of all comers to Kents should be a model of courtesy, interest and helpfulness. Your manner and appearance must inspire confidence and create a feeling which is in accord with Kents tradition of warm-heartedness allied with dignity, of pleasantness with efficiency.'

Menswear department – at Kents men could chose whether to buy their suit off-the-peg or have it tailor-made

29

Making tubes of fruit pastilles before the days of conveyor belts

Conveyor belts speeded up production. They were first used by Henry Ford to make cars in the USA

In the factory

Bill Francis remembers that there were many changes in the sweet factory during these years.

Bill:

'To me it seemed like the age of the conveyor belt. We hadn't had them before the war. Now, everywhere you looked there were rows of sweets moving along, perhaps to be coated in sugar or chocolate, or to be wrapped, ready for the shops. Just about every process was automated – apart from eating them!'

During the 1950s wages rose very quickly, as these figures show:

Average weekly wage of a man employed in a manufacturing industry

1950	£ 7.71
1955	£11.39
1960	£14.99

Unemployment was very low (under 2%) and some areas didn't have enough people to fill all the job vacancies. In 1984 unemployment in Britain was about 14.25%. The 1950s also saw fewer strikes than at any time since, and there seemed no reason for people to worry about their future at work.

Women's work

The sort of office which Jean worked in

Most wives and mothers with young children in the 1950s didn't go out to work.

Eileen:
'I didn't work when my children were young, and women who did choose to work when they had small children, were really rather disapproved of by some people. My neighbour, Jean Francis, decided to take a part-time job when her daughter, Valerie, started secondary school in 1956. This seems perfectly sensible now, but I can remember being a bit surprised by Jean's daring decision!'

Jean found work five mornings a week in the offices of the sweet factory where her husband, Bill, was a section manager.

Jean:
'I worked at a desk in a really plain, big room. The floor was just wooden floorboards, and the walls were painted cream, with no pictures. Quite a few people worked in the office, and the desks were placed close together. Sometimes it was difficult to work, especially if the person next to you was typing or having a telephone conversation.'

31

The Welfare State

By the 1950s Britain was becoming known as a 'Welfare State'. Most people could now claim financial benefits in the case of accident, illness or unemployment.

Edward:
'It seemed marvellous to have all these new privileges. It was a great relief to most people to be able to consult a doctor without having to pay a hefty bill. In the days before sick pay, being seriously ill or laid off work with an injury often meant disaster for the whole family.'

The new benefits were paid for in part by National Insurance contributions, which were deducted by the government from wages and employers. The National Health Service, which started in 1948, gave everyone the right to free medical treatment. The NHS also made available free false teeth and spectacles. Dentists became booked up for months ahead in the early years of the NHS, and National Health spectacle frames soon became a familiar sight. There was also a National Health wig, which can't have been too convincing as it was very easily recognised!

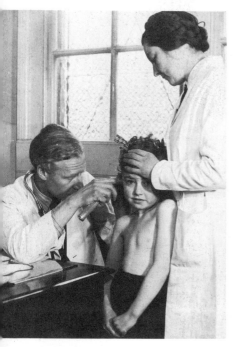

Each school child had an eye and hearing test

Health visitors were appointed by the NHS to visit people at home

Better conditions at work

Working hours changed for the better. Before the war, most people were employed for five and a half or six days a week, often putting in ten or eleven hours a day.

Edward:
'I remember my father always worked a six day week. Even when my own working week was cut to five days, and our working day officially finished at six o'clock, there was often extra work to be done, and we thought nothing of staying on until it was finished.'

By the end of the 1950s, the five day working week of eight hours a day was being adopted by more employers. Staff canteens, comfortable cloakrooms and even such facilities as recreation rooms began to be provided. In many pre-war factories there had not even been anywhere for staff to eat their lunch.

Before the war, not many people were entitled to holidays with pay. Edward had one week's paid holiday when he returned to Kents after the war, and this was increased to two weeks during the 1950s. By the end of the 1950s most working people had a fortnight's paid leave.

33

Holidays

People began to look for more adventurous things to do in their holidays. In the past, families who could afford holidays had often made for seaside resorts like Margate and Blackpool, staying in boarding houses or hotels.

The new family caravans were a different and fairly cheap way to take a holiday. Caravan sites became a familiar sight in the countryside and at seaside resorts.

Holiday camps became very popular in the 1950s. They offered entertainment-packed, reasonably priced family holidays, and were an enormous success.

John:

'I remember my Uncle Robert coming back from Butlins, saying what a wonderful holiday it had been, and telling us all about the funfairs, swimming pools and competitions they had there. I really wanted to go to a holiday camp, and I wasn't disappointed when Mum and Dad took us to Pontins. It was fantastic – there were things to do all the time.'

Bill boards advertising outings

34

Summer on Brighton beach, 1957

Many families went hop picking in Kent for their summer holidays. It was a good way of enjoying the sunshine and earning some extra money

35

6　Television and teenagers

Radios, or 'wireless sets' as they used to be known, had been common since before the war.

John:
'*The Goon Show* and *The Navy Lark* were both very popular radio comedy shows. I can remember lots of friends at school talking in the funny voices used by the Goons – it almost became a way of life for some people! We had a copy of the Goon record, *The Ying Tong Song*. It was hilarious – I must have nearly worn it out, I played it so much.'

In 1954, radio programmes had audiences of about nine million people. Only three years later, audiences were down by two thirds. This sudden drop was because of television.

Television broadcasts had started before the war, but all such services were suspended during the war years. When television started up again, it had an enormous impact on family life. At first television was treated as a novelty, and it wasn't until 1953 that it really became popular. Audiences soared for the broadcast of the Coronation – 25 million people watched. Television was here to stay. It was like a miracle to see real people moving and talking, real events taking place on that little screen in your own sitting room, even though they were only in black and white.

Recording a radio broadcast of the Goon Show: left to right, Spike Milligan, Peter Sellers and Harry Secombe

What's My Line? presented by Eamonn Andrews. Even off-screen announcers and technicians wore smart evening dress

At first there was just one channel, the BBC, and not many viewing hours each day. Programmes stopped between 6 and 7 o'clock, so that children could be put to bed! Television closed down at 10.30 pm, and through the day there were many gaps or 'interludes' between programmes, when people could watch restful pictures of things like a potter's wheel.

There was a big rush to buy sets in 1955, after the introduction of ITV, the new commercial channel.

Quiz shows involving the audience started to be broadcast after the introduction of ITV. The Turners remember enjoying *Take your Pick* and *Double your Money*. Serials, especially those with medical themes, were great favourites. Ask someone in your family if they remember *Emergency Ward Ten* or *The Grove Family*.

Sandra:
'I was thrilled when, at last, we got a TV. My favourite programme was *6.5 Special*, a programme of jiving and rock'n'roll music.'

Some films always bring in the crowds. In the Fifties, British war films and the Ealing Comedies, like 'Kind Hearts and Coronets' were great favourites

As more and more people watched TV, cinema audiences declined. Between 1954 and 1959 more than 800 cinemas were forced to close. Even so, for many people a trip to the pictures was still the treat of the week.

John:
'I often went to the Saturday morning 'flicks' – film shows specially for children. Later on, I used to like horror films – things like Dracula or Frankenstein. Something that's completely gone today is the cinema newsreel. This was the only way of seeing the news before we had a TV.'

Valerie Francis, the daughter of the Turners' neighbours, was a teenager in the 1950s.

Valerie:
'I remember reading film magazines, full of pin-ups of film stars like Marilyn Monroe and James Dean, and news and stories about the stars and their latest films. The cinema seemed much more glamorous then than it does today.'

Dancing

About five million people went ballroom dancing each week. Jean and Bill Francis used to go to the local Locarno ballroom right through the 1950s. Thousands of teenagers, including Valerie Francis, went to ballroom dancing lessons.

Valerie:
'I used to like the names of the dances we were taught, the Square Tango, the Cha-cha, the Veleta. My 13 year old daughter tells me that she's never heard of the Veleta, but she thinks it sounds like a sort of cheese!'

Most songs, before about 1955, were aimed at older people, and were often sung by 'crooners' like Bing Crosby and Frankie Vaughan. Otherwise, songs were for small children, with words like 'Rudolph the red-nosed reindeer had a very shiny nose . . .'. Children went from nursery rhymes to the music of their parents with nothing in between.

The word 'teenager' was first used in the 1950s. For the first time, young people had money to spend, because of full employment and increases in wages. Suddenly there were new kinds of music to listen to; rock'n'roll, skiffle and lively bands which appealed to teenagers.

Couples from amateur clubs dancing to Victor Sylvester's band

In 1955 'Rock around the clock' exploded into the pop music charts. With its fast, pounding rhythm and energetic tune, it stayed at the Number 1 position for many weeks. There was no looking back, never again would the Top Ten be dominated by the older generation's favourites.

By the end of the decade, rock'n'roll singers like Elvis Presley, Jerry Lee Lewis and Little Richard, were being idolised by millions of teenagers all over the world. There was a new wave of British pop stars too, like Tommy Steele and Marty Wilde.

The music was fast, exciting and with a strong beat. Best of all, it was just for the young.

1959 – Marty Wilde's hit 'Donna' reached no.3 in the Hit Parade

Teenagers jiving on the BBC's 6:05 Special – the first music show for young people

If you wanted to chat to friends or dance to rock'n'roll records you might go to the Youth Club. But most young people liked to meet in coffee bars. Teenagers went there to drink Italian-style, foamy Espresso coffee – and to listen to the latest records on the juke box.

Valerie Francis:
'I remember how daring and rebellious I felt going to coffee bars. They were something new and different – places for teenagers to meet one another. The older generation were definitely excluded! We thought we were really "with it", so "cool" and in step with all the latest fashions. Those who didn't fit in, we simply wrote off as "squares".'

When the bars first opened, hundreds of people used to queue outside, listening to the thumping of the juke box just for a few minutes.

The early coffee bars were often jammed full, with queues outside. Inside, people drank milk or espresso coffee

Early Matchbox toys

Toys, sweets and comics

In the 1950s the number and variety of toys was better than ever before.

Angela:
'Dolls became much more realistic while I was little. I remember when baby dolls that actually wet themselves came into the shops – I thought they were amazing! When I was older I got one of the new "teenage" dolls, and spent hours combing her hair and dressing her up in different, fashionable clothes.'

John;
'I had lots of Dinky and Matchbox cars, and a Meccano construction set. Oh, and one thing I loved to play in was my cowboy outfit. I used to terrorise my sisters and their friends with my gun.'

When he was ten, John got 2/- (10p) a week pocket money. As soon as he could, he put his name down for a paper round, to earn some extra money. At the end of the 1950s Ron Atkins, who ran the local newsagent's shop, remembers paying his newspaper boys and girls 7/6 (38p) for a weekly round.

Some of the children's money went on sweets. Many sweets that were enjoyed then are no longer made. Sandra remembers a bar called 'Nux', and John loved the 'Five Boys' chocolate bar, neither of which are manufactured today.

Joyce Atkins, at the newsagent's shop, remembers the end of sweet rationing in 1954 and the different varieties of packaged bars and sweets that began to come into the shop.

Joyce:
'Before the 1950s, most of the sweets were in jars or big boxes and there was a lot more weighing out and putting in bags than today. Many of the children coming in would just want 2 oz ($3\frac{1}{2}$ g) of their favourite acid drops, bull's eyes or whatever. When all the new packaged bars and sweets were being introduced, the sales representatives from the big firms, like Rowntrees and Cadburys, would leave samples for us to try out first. Our son, Ian, thought this was great, and some of his friends, like Angela Turner, were quite pleased to help us taste the new sweets as well!'

Some toys and sweets haven't changed much since the Fifties

Children choosing books at their local library

Children's annuals

John, Sandra and Angela looked forward to Wednesday mornings, when their comics were delivered with the newspaper.

At the beginning of the 1950s both boys' and girls' comics were full of tales about boarding school life. Soon, boys' comics like *Eagle* began to introduce new features like space adventures and historical stories. Cartoon strips featured favourites like *Tiger Tim and the Bruin Boys, Beryl the Peril*, and, of course, *Desperate Dan* and the *Bash Street Kids*. For girls there was *Girl*, and *Bunty*, which first came out in 1958.

Teenage magazines began at the end of the 1950s, with *Boyfriend* starting in 1959. This was followed by several others such as *Valentine*, all of which sold in large numbers.

Books

The Turner family used the public library service a great deal. In the years 1959 and 1960 the number of public libraries in Britain doubled.

Sandra:
'We used to have a weekly outing to the library on Friday evenings, when it was open late. The whole family went, and we came away with piles of books. I used to love getting home and taking my new books upstairs to look at them more closely. My favourites were the Famous Five Books.'

Book sales increased during this period. By 1958 sales of paperback books, which had very plain covers in those days, had reached 60 million a year. Before the war they had sold about 10 million each year.

Millions of books were sold through mail order book clubs. These clubs concentrated on fiction, and the books they offered were all bound in the same way. Today, the Turners still have rows of identically bound books from book clubs.

Sport

After years of shortages and restrictions, people were determined to enjoy themselves. The Turners and their friends remember that there were many new things to do in their spare time during these years.

Edward's favourite sport then was fishing – and it still is today. In the 1950s, two million people went fishing regularly. This was, perhaps surprisingly, far more than the number who played football seriously – about three-quarters of a million. There were nearly three thousand amateur football teams playing in local Sunday leagues. Football League matches were well attended, and from 1950 onwards Britain took part in the World Cup.

Players and spectators at a Sunday morning football match on Blackheath Common in London

There was great interest in important tennis tournaments like the one held at Wimbledon each year. Tennis was a favourite sport to play as well as to watch.

Eileen:
'There seemed to be many new courts appearing at that time. In 1950 Oakley got some really good new tennis courts. It cost 6d (2½p) to play there for half an hour.'

Popular sports personalities included Freddie Trueman the cricketer, and Roger Bannister, the first man to run the mile in less than four minutes. In 1954, a British athlete, Diane Leather, became the first woman in the world to run the mile in less than five minutes.

Roger Bannister broke the four minute mile in 1954

17 year old Little Mo from the US beats Angela Mortimer from Britain at Wimbledon 1952

7 Fifties fashions

During the war years, there were hardly any new clothes in the shops. There had been a severe shortage of material, and of people to make the material into clothes. Clothes rationing lasted until 1949, which meant that each person was issued with a small number of coupons with which to buy new clothes.

Eileen:
'We spent a lot of time mending clothes at home, to make everything last as long as possible. I'll never forget the sight of my young brother going to school in a coat that nearly reached his ankles! It had been given to him by our neighbours – people then were always passing on clothes which had been grown out of, to friends or relations. Nothing was thrown out until it had dropped to bits!'

Wartime clothes were practical and hardwearing. The Utility scheme, which lasted until 1952, controlled the quality of clothing but there were not many styles to choose from.

Models show off the 1955 fashions. Even in hot weather women often wore hats and seamed stockings

Austere utility dresses

"Aberdeen's Foremost Fashion House"

UTILITY DRESSES
by three of the most Famous Designers

jersey de luxe

Price 82/2

Price 60/-

jersey de luxe

rembrant

Price 60/-

hollywood

Price 53/7

WATT & GRANT, LTD. UNION ST. ABERDEEN

47

Model wearing the 'New Look' style coat

The New Look

During wartime women wore suits with square shoulders and knee length narrow skirts. In 1947 the famous 'New Look' was launched by Christian Dior. This fashion, with its extravagant use of material, was a direct contrast to the wartime 'look', and was criticised by many people at the time when clothes rationing and the Utility scheme were still part of everyday life. Eileen and her friends liked the new fashion, and as soon as they could afford to buy more clothes, they began to wear the 'New Look'. For everyday wear women chose classic styles, designed to last a long time.

Eileen:
'I would almost always wear a tweed skirt and a twin set or cardigan and blouse in winter. In summer we had cotton dresses with full skirts and narrow waists.'

Hats and gloves, particularly in the early 1950s, were an essential part of a woman's and a little girl's wardrobe. No one would have been considered really smartly dressed without gloves or a hat. Extravagant and outrageous hats were often the focus of attention in fashion magazines.

Eileen and her friend Joyce

Dresses in shop window display – polka dots and stripes were very 'in'

Children's clothes

In the 1950s you would not have found children wearing jeans or dungarees, as they do today. Little girls wore cotton dresses with full skirts, and cardigans, in summer. In winter they would wear warm pleated skirts or kilts (often with a bodice attached), usually with cardigans again. Tartan trousers, known as trews, were popular. In the days before central heating most children wore a lot of underwear. Both Turner girls remember wearing what were called 'liberty bodices'. These were like thick, warm vests (but usually worn *over* a vest!).

For occasions when they had to be smartly dressed, girls were expected to wear hats.

Sandra:
'I hated having to wear a hat for Sunday School. It used to drive me mad – I was so uncomfortable. I could hardly wait to get home so I could get the thing off my head!'

Girls wore socks well into their teens, and an important mark of growing up was when a girl began to wear stockings, usually held up by a suspender belt. People called the new, fashionable stockings 'nylons' after the material they were made of.

Children's clothes were more formal than they are today

John in his best overcoat

Penny for the Guy

Boys wore short trousers, even in the coldest weather, until they were at secondary school at least. The change to long trousers for boys marked an important stage in life, rather like the change from socks to stockings for girls. Knee-length socks (held up with garters), thick, belted, gaberdine coats and heavy lace-up shoes were part of the wardrobes of most boys. Wearing a duffle coat to school was very daring and usually not allowed.

John:
'Nearly all my clothes when I was small seemed to be grey. My "short" trousers and socks were both so long that only a bit of knee showed in between! I remember wearing bala-clava helmets that my gran had knitted me, in winter – only a small circle of nose, eyes and mouth peeped out from all the wool!'

Small boys almost always had short back and sides haircuts. Little girls' hair was usually shoulder or neck length, with a parting, and hair ribbons and slides. The emphasis was on neatness.

Teenage fashion

For the first time ever, there were special fashions for teenagers and young people. Teenage girls started to wear chunky-knit sweaters and slacks or full, bouncy skirts, with lots of stiff net petticoats underneath – marvellous for dancing rock'n'roll. At school, girls used to try to squash their starched petticoats under their uniform.

The fashion for stiletto-heeled shoes, with pointed toes, was responsible for ruining many floors and carpets. Sometimes you would see notices in public buildings asking any ladies wearing stiletto-heeled shoes to remove them before entering. Special overshoes with large heels were sometimes provided, to prevent damage by stiletto heels. Some fashionable shoes were called 'winkle pickers' because of their pointed toes.

Beatniks first appeared in the Fifties. They were people who liked to be thought of as intellectuals and poets. The men wore beards and long straggly hair, and used to look 'cool' in black rollneck jumpers. Girls borrowed their boyfriends' jumpers.

Eileen in her slacks

Fifties fashions for women usually came in to a tight waist, often emphasised by a belt, with a flared skirt

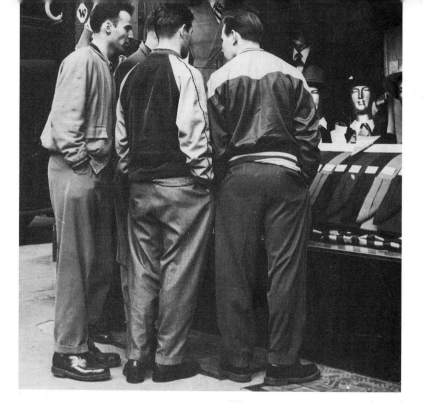

Fifties clothes were influenced by fashions from abroad. These men have copied American styles. Italian-looking clothes were also popular

Teddy boys wore tight trousers, narrow ties and long jackets trimmed with velvet. They were always very careful to dress smartly

Some young men liked to dress as 'Teddy Boys'. This fashion, started by rich young men in the West End of London, was an exaggerated version of the Edwardian look – narrow trousers (called 'drainpipes'), velvet-collared jackets and brocade waistcoats.

Not all young men followed the Teddy Boy fashion. Most men wore a suit to work and on formal occasions; sports jackets and flannels were favourite wear at weekends. A tie was almost always worn and great numbers of men still wore a hat, though the bowler was seen less often except in the City and at funerals.

Nowadays everyone is used to wearing shirts and blouses of man-made fibres like polyester, but in the 1950s nylon and terylene were only just appearing.

Eileen:
'It was a great novelty to have drip-dry clothes for the first time. With all the dresses I had to wash for Sandra and Angela, it was a pleasure to be able to miss out the ironing stage!'

A much wider range of high quality mass-produced clothing was available than in previous years, which meant that more people could afford to dress well.

Hairstyles

Hairstyles had not changed much for many years. Many men used haircream to keep their hair looking slick and neat. Women in the early 1950s would quite often have tightly permed hair. It was fashionable to copy the hairstyles worn by filmstars. The film 'Roman Holiday' was released in 1953. It starred Audrey Hepburn who wore a short elfin hairstyle. Soon afterwards a lot of women were copying the style.

Later in the 1950s young women started to grow their hair longer again, and one fashion was to tie the hair back into a pony-tail.

Some men began to wear quite complicated hairstyles. Teddy boys used to favour a style called a DA. They slicked their hair back with cream and left a little curl at the back like a drake's tail.

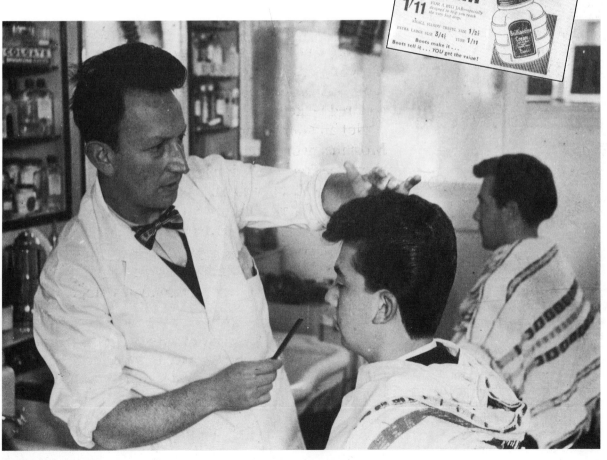

At the hairdresser

John's school photograph

8   John, Sandra and Angela at school

A great many changes had taken place in schools, as a result of an Act of Parliament passed in 1944. This Act aimed to provide a better education for all children. However, there were still not enough teachers, buildings or equipment to meet the needs of all the children of school age.

Some schools had been destroyed or badly damaged in air raids. After the war, the Government launched a massive school building programme, but this at first concentrated on building secondary schools. Many primary schools were still very overcrowded.

John:
'Newton Street School, where we went, was an old Victorian building that had been bomb-damaged during the war, but the main problem was that it was far too small. Lots of prefabricated huts had been put up in the playground, to cope with all the pupils. This used up a lot of space, and there wasn't much room left for us to play in. In the classroom, we had to share huge, ink-stained battered desks.'

Classroom at a village primary school. In the Fifties teachers first started using less formal methods of education, and helped young children to learn through play

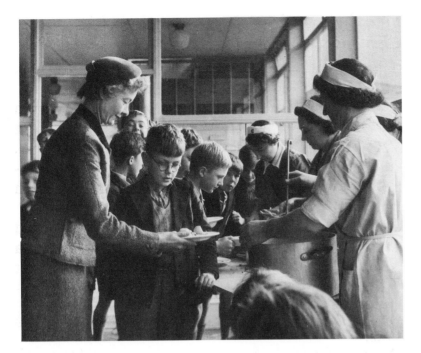

School milk seems to hold vivid memories for many children of the 1950s.

Sandra:
'I was a milk monitor. Each teacher chose two children in the class for this job, which involved handing out the milk and straws to all the pupils in the class, at playtime.'

John can recall the milk being delivered to the school in crates full of third of a pint bottles, which were stacked against the school wall. Angela's memories of school milk are not very happy.

Angela:
'In summer the milk was horribly luke-warm, and in winter the bottles were sometimes put next to a radiator to thaw the contents. We were made to drink it. I never drink milk by itself now.'

School dinners were taken by most of the children at Newton Street School.

John:
'I remember that school dinners cost 1/- (5p) each day. It was usually meat and two veg., followed by a hot pudding covered in custard, which I used to love – as long as the custard wasn't too lumpy!'

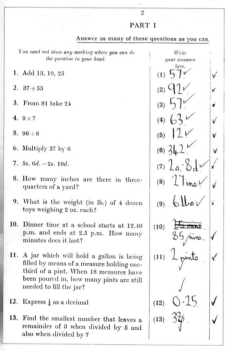

What I would do if I had Aladdins lamp. Well first I would have a few wishes like having a two wheeler bicle which I have never been able to have because of busy roads and a few other things for mummy and daddy.

I would also stop all kind of wars which are going, and stop the ones for the future. As well I would stop all the people (scientists) from making these horible bombs which are the main cause of these wars.

Also I would rub Aladdins lamp, and wish that no one would ever be beggers.

2

PART I

Answer as many of these questions as you can.

You need not show any working where you can do the question in your head.

Write your answers here.

1. Add 13, 19, 25 — (1) 57 ✓
2. 37 + 55 — (2) 92 ✓
3. From 81 take 24 — (3) 57 ✓
4. 9 × 7 — (4) 63 ✓
5. 96 ÷ 8 — (5) 12 ✓
6. Multiply 57 by 6 — (6) 342 ✓
7. 5s. 6d. − 2s. 10d. — (7) 2s. 8d ✓
8. How many inches are there in three-quarters of a yard? — (8) 27 ins ✓
9. What is the weight (in lb.) of 4 dozen toys weighing 2 oz. each? — (9) 6 lbs ✓
10. Dinner time at a school starts at 12.40 p.m. and ends at 2.5 p.m. How many minutes does it last? — (10) 85 mins. ✓
11. A jar which will hold a gallon is being filled by means of a measure holding one-third of a pint. When 18 measures have been poured in, how many pints are still needed to fill the jar? — (11) 2 pints ✓
12. Express ¼ as a decimal — (12) 0·25 ✓
13. Find the smallest number that leaves a remainder of 3 when divided by 5 and also when divided by 7 — (13) 38 ✓

11 Plus papers

Most primary schools had formal writing lessons, when children copied out rows of the same letter in careful handwriting

56

Some subjects, like history and geography, were taught in a very formal way, with the teacher telling the pupils facts, which were then written down in exercise books. However, many teachers were beginning to realise that if children's interest could be aroused and they could be encouraged to look things up for themselves, far more would be learnt.

In primary schools there was often a strong emphasis on good handwriting. Children learned to write using a wooden pen with a metal nib, which frequently had to be dipped into an ink-pot. Later on, they might be allowed to use a fountain pen with a special nib. Sometimes pupils were taught to write in a particular style.

Sandra:

'We were taught italic handwriting at Newton Street school. I found it satisfying to produce a page of beautiful neat writing. My handwriting today still shows the influence of italic script quite clearly.'

Radio broadcasts specially for schools were still quite a new idea at this time.

A school outing to the theatre

Angela:
'There was a musical programme that we used to listen to. We had BBC booklets to use in the lesson, with the words and music of the songs in them. We giggled a bit at first – it seemed a strange thing to do at school.'

Teachers in the 1950s were quite formal and strict.

John:
'I found arithmetic very difficult. We were just bombarded with rules. I couldn't seem to understand it at all. To make it worse I was so scared of the teacher that I didn't dare ask him to explain anything to me again.'

For most lessons pupils sat at their desks, watching the teacher at the blackboard. Even quite young children had to follow a timetable of lessons.

Sandra:
'There were very strict rules about behaviour. If a teacher caught you running in the corridor, it meant extra work for you – during playtime! Caning was quite common, I think a lot of children were frightened into behaving themselves properly.'

Secondary modern class, 1959

One of the biggest hurdles for primary school children was the 11 Plus. This was an examination that most children had to sit, to decide what sort of secondary school they would go to. There was a lot of pressure on children to do well in this exam.

In the 1950s there were two main types of secondary school: grammar schools and secondary moderns. In grammar schools children were expected to study for examinations. Secondary moderns offered more practical subjects like art, craft and cookery. Although they were supposed to be equal, almost everyone thought the grammar schools were 'better' because they accepted the cleverest children.

John:
'As soon as the 11 Plus results became known, it was a "them and us" situation. I failed the exam so I went on to the secondary modern school. On the bus that took us from Oakley to Moreton, where the secondary schools were, the grammar school pupils would sit in one part, the secondary modern pupils in another. It was horrible, really; there was such a division between the two groups.'

58

Secondary modern schools, because they did not place so much importance on examination results, were able to explore new ways of making lessons more interesting and exciting.

Valerie Francis:
'Dressmaking classes were made far more absorbing than they used to be. We designed our own clothes and even dyed and printed our own material.'

Secondary moderns also experimented with project work, which all school children do nowadays, and also with outings to places of interest. Some secondary modern schools took school trips abroad.

John:
'Journeys abroad with your school were something very new and different. My parents had never been abroad, but they made a big effort to save enough money, so that I could go. A group of us went skiing in Switzerland with some teachers. It was a wonderful experience – I don't think I ever enjoyed a week so much!'

Eileen:
'Sometimes, we wondered what on earth the children were learning at school. They always seemed to be one step ahead of us.'

Learning how to use a mangle and iron in a housecraft lesson

Clay modelling in an art class

9 The space age

The space race was often front page news in the Fifties

Perhaps the most exciting venture of the 1950s was the launching of the first satellite into outer space. John remembers what a stir this caused.

John:
'When we heard in autumn 1957 that two Sputniks had been launched into outer space by the Russians, it seemed like a story from a science fiction film. We learnt all about it at school. I think we found it difficult to imagine that a rocket had actually sent something into orbit round the earth.'

By March 1958, America had launched her third earth satellite. The space race had started. One month later, the Soviet Sputnik II disintegrated over the Caribbean. It had completed 2370 circuits of the earth and had travelled 62 million miles.

Edward:
'The Space Age had arrived. The 1950s had been busy years for my family, and years that seemed full of changes in the world. With all the new developments that had happened so quickly, I think Eileen and I realised even then that by the time our children had grown up, the world would be a very different place.'

A Giles cartoon, from the Sunday Express, 1957

"Fire Brigade? We wish to report we've just launched Sputnik 3."

Sunday Express, November 10th, 1957

More books to read

Growing Up in the 1950s by C.A.R. Hills (Batsford, 1983)
Growing Up in the Fifties by Jeremy Pascall (Wayland, 1980)

This book is for slightly older readers:
The Fifties by Peter Lewis (Heinemann, 1978)

Two story books which tell you about family life in the 1950s:
Box for Benny by Leila Berg (Magnet, 1983)
Magnolia Buildings by Elizabeth Stucley (Penguin, 1965)

Acknowledgements

Associated Newspapers Group pages 6 (left), 17 (bottom), 36 (top)
Barnaby's Picture Library pages 9 (top), 62
BBC pages 36 (bottom), 37
BBC Hulton Picture Library pages 9 (bottom), 10, 16, 26 (bottom), 38 (top), 39, 40, (right), 45, 51 (bottom), 53 (bottom)
Beamish Museum pages 14 (bottom right), 25, 38 (bottom), 44 (top), 49 (top), 50, 52 (left)
Boots Ltd page 53 (top)
Coop pages 19, 21, 57
Design Council Picture Library page 13 (bottom)
John Frost Historical Newspaper Service pages 34 (left), 60
Henry Grant pages 3, 12, 28 (bottom), 32, 34 (right), 35, 41, 47 (top), 52 (right), 54 (bottom), 55, 56 (right), 58, 59, 63
Greater London Council Record Office page 56 (left)
House of Fraser pages 22, 29, 47 (bottom), 48 (bottom right)
Alison Hurst pages 5 (bottom), 7, 8 (top left), 26 (top), 27 (top), 48, 49 (bottom), 51 (top), 54 (top)
London Express Newspaper and Feature Services page 60
National Dairy Council page 20 (top)
Pollocks Toy Museum pages 42, 43 (left)
Popperfoto pages 1, 24, 28 (top), 46, 48 (top)
Proctor & Gamble page 14 (bottom left)
David Redfern – cover photo
Rowntree Mackintosh pages 30, 43 (middle and right)
J. Sainsbury PLC pages 5 (top), 33, 53
Thorn EMI Electric page 13 (top)
Topical Press page 6 (right)
United Dairies page 20 (bottom)
Wimpey Homes Holdings Ltd pages 8 (right), 11, 15 (left), 17 (top), 18 (top), 31
Woolworths page 23

Some facts and figures from the 1950s

1950
Population of Great Britain about 44.5 million
Labour government in power – Clement Attlee Prime Minister
USSR declares it has built an atomic bomb
Petrol rationing ended
The first plastic records imported from the USA – replacing the heavy '78' records
350 000 homes in Britain have a television
Start of Korean war.

1951
Conservative government comes to power, with Winston Churchill as Prime Minister
Average weekly earnings of man over 21 are £8 6s (£8.30)
Festival of Britain held in May
1.5 million households have a private telephone
GCE examinations introduced
Stiletto heeled shoes become fashionable
The Archers radio serial begins

1952
King George VI dies in February
Identity cards abolished in Britain
Britain explodes its own test atomic bomb (and becomes the third nuclear power, after the USA and the USSR)
First jet airliner service operated from London to Johannesburg
Return air fare from London to Scotland is £8
The Goon Show begins on radio
The play, *The Mousetrap*, opens in London's West End

1953
Coronation of Queen Elizabeth II in June
Mount Everest climbed by Hillary and Tensing
England wins the Ashes at the Oval for the first time in 27 years
Publication of *Casino Royale*, the first James Bond novel, by Ian Fleming
About 3 million homes now have a television

1954
Most food rationing ends
Crime rate lowest since the war
USA H-bomb tested at Bikini Atoll
Roger Bannister becomes the first person to run a mile in less than 4 minutes
Diane Leather breaks the women's record by running a mile in less than 5 minutes
Films – *On the Waterfront* starring Marlon Brando
Rear Window directed by Alfred Hitchcock

1955
Sir Anthony Eden succeeds Churchill as Prime Minister
Ruth Ellis is the last woman to be hanged in Britain
First ITV broadcast
Rock'n'roll arrives in England
First Espresso coffee bars open in London
Diesel trains begin to replace the old steam locomotives
Films –*Rebel without a cause* starring James Dean
Rock around the clock with Bill Haley

Dancing at the local club

A class of primary school children

1956
First British nuclear power station opens at Calder Hall
Trans-Atlantic telephone service begins
Clean Air Act to prevent smog – no more coal fires allowed in London
Rock'n'roll grows in popularity
Tommy Steele rises to fame
Elvis Presley's first record *Heartbreak Hotel* released
8% of households have refrigerators
Meat rationing ends (last of food rationing)
Suez crisis between Britain, France and Egypt

1957
British H-bomb tested at Christmas Island
USSR launches first earth satellite – Sputnik I – in October
Hula hoop craze reaches a peak
Teenagers queue to see Skiffle bands
Over 1000 Espresso bars in Britian
'Squares' a popular slang expression
First year that as many people crossed the Atlantic by plane as by ship

1958
Common Market formed but Britain not included
CND established – first Aldermaston march in April
Traffic wardens and parking meters appear in London
First tower blocks erected in Britain
Manchester United loses 7 players in Munich air crash
Civil Service introduces equal pay for women
First direct long distance telephone calls without using the operator
Blue Peter children's television programme begins

1959
Population of Great Britain about 46 million
M1 opened – first motorway in Britain
The Mini car introduced
Rock'n'roll star Buddy Holly killed in air crash
Juke Box Jury started – TV panel programme on pop music
Over 9 million homes in Britain have a television

Index